ROY CONNOR

THE GREATEST YOU

**The Ultimate Guide on How to Become a More
Effective Person, Learn Proven Methods on How
to Improve Yourself and Become the Greatest You**

Descrierea CIP a Bibliotecii Naţionale a României
ROY CONNOR
    THE GREATEST YOU. The Ultimate Guide on How to Become a More Effective Person, Learn Proven Methods on How to Improve Yourself and Become the Greatest You / Roy Connor – Bucharest: Editura My Ebook, 2021
    ISBN

ROY CONNOR

THE GREATEST YOU

**The Ultimate Guide on How to Become a More
Effective Person, Learn Proven Methods on How
to Improve Yourself and Become the Greatest You**

My Ebook Publishing House
Bucharest, 2021

TABLE OF CONTENTS

Chapter 1

The Basics of Effectiveness

Synopsis

People are facing different challenges in their daily lives. They need to come up with good results to prove themselves or somebody else that they are worthy of doing so. Basically, these tasks are evaluated according to their degree of effectiveness and efficiency. Whether you are in a business owner, an employee, or an ordinary person at home, it is highly essential to management effectiveness well.

The overall success of what you are currently doing depends how you will get things done right. For this reason, you need to learn what it is all about and how it can totally affect your personality and the things around you.

Bear in mind that the final outcome of what you had done will reflect to you as a person. Thus, you must think and follow what is right naturally. If you want to improve your perception about effectiveness, continue reading and put into your mind and heart all the information you are going to learn.

What is Effectiveness?

Effectiveness refers to the degree in which objectives have been obtained and the extent which target problems have been resolved. It is distinguished with no reference to cost. Effectiveness also means "doing the right thing while efficiency is about "doing such thing right". Another definition that may be incorporated with this word is the ability of intervention to perform more good things than harm for target population in the real world situation.

Personal effectiveness is not all about reaching your goals for you can do it in a time consuming, sloppy, or wasteful way. It implies that you have to start making use of time practically as well as the rest of personal resources. This is how you achieve goals efficiently, such as investment, and get the best return.

Effective individuals are more than those persons who obtain what they exactly want. These people have 2 qualities: They are making the best use of resources and they have been skilled at reaching their goals. Regardless of your main purpose in life, being effective indicates a good combination of skilled execution and efficiency.

People have been personally effective in distinct ways. This is due to the fact that everybody has various values, priorities, and goals in life. For instance, skilled communicators are effective in various ways according to what they wish to achieve. Some individuals who wish to entertain others should have an exceptional sense of humor. Once they impressed a broad audience, then they posses incredible presentation skills. On the other hand, the coach has to become a good listener and communicate sensitively.

Key Themes of Effectiveness

- **Reliable** – consistent, predictable, supports "single truth source", self- correcting
- **Appropriate** – optimizes support and supports for business purposes
- **Elegant** – simplicity, self adapting, clarity, consistency for various human factors
- **Integrated** – supports, creates, and optimizes synergy in the entire systems

- **Efficient** – minimizes resource wastage and optimizes resource use

Effectiveness takes place when all things support everything else. When talking about business, many organizations are focused on giving exerting more efforts for efficiency. Efficiency is just a dimension of the entire effectiveness. To achieve exceptional results, all elements should be managed properly, fairly and consistently.

Chapter 2

Be Proactive

Synopsis

As part of obtaining effectiveness as a person, you have to understand how to be proactive. Being proactive is about taking responsibility when it comes to your actions and life than simply watching how such things happen and pass by. It actually takes time because you need to consider the available options. You need to learn to weigh alternatives wisely and make an informed decision to reach your goals in life. The "reactive" behavior has been influenced by outside forces and environmental factors.

An individual's proactive behavior or proactivity refers to change-oriented, self-initiated and anticipatory behavior in a particular situation, such as in a workplace. Proactive behavior includes acting on a future situation in advance than simply reacting. This means taking control of things and making them happen than waiting for things to happen or adjusting to such situation.

Proactive behavior has been contrasted with some work-related behaviors, like proficiency or adaptivity. Adaptivity refers to change response, while proactivity refers to change initiation. Proactivity has not been restricted to additional role performance behavior.

How to be Proactive?

As you face your daily chances, there have been 2 key approaches to take the necessary action. The first one is the reactive approach, and the other one is the proactive approach.

Proactive approach has been an alternative to reactive action-taking. In this approach, you have to determine the tasks (actions) in advanced .These are the tasks you will take in the entire day. However, at times, you need to stay flexible for some unexpected occurrences. Proactive action-taking has been characterized by providing a possible action thought while making decisions consciously.

The truth is that there are more people who use the reactive action-taking approach than a proactive one. Still, it is possible and straightforward to change an approach. This is how to do it:

- *Faith in Proactive behavior* – the first step is having a mental transformation of what you have believed. To be a proactive action- taker, believe that it will work.

- *Personal Action Plan* – PAP has three initial sections which are comprised of ghost actions, minor actions, and major actions. In order to make it simpler, determine 3 main actions you wanted to do within a day. In the mean time, forget about other ghost or minor actions. Take them on the next part of the process.

- *Focus on Your Action* – After identifying the big actions, start by accomplishing one at a time. Stay for a while and take a break for refreshment. Come back and do the next task. Take these steps until you accomplish the other items on the list.

- *Avoid reactive triggers* – it can be difficult not to fall back to your previous behaviors. Give your best to get rid of reactive action taking through avoiding some common factors around you or the previous things you used to do. Focus on the 3 things you have identified. Do not allow anybody else to ruin your day and your mindset.

- *Be firm* – If you were not used to do so, the proactive approach might be quite odd for you, especially when you were previously a reactive action-taker. Have some time in changing your approach. Never fight against yourself and go back to the old ways. The best thing to do is to go back to being proactive and do better continuously.

To be proactive also indicates anticipating problems, giving your best and finding new solutions. On the contrary, being reactive means resolving problems when turned up, performing minimum effort, and disliking changes. Being proactive is having clear thoughts about personal goals and carrying out right actions to make these goals achievable.

Chapter 3

Clarify Your Goals

Synopsis

Goals provide the direction while it helps a person spend his time constructively. Adjust and change your goals regularly. Goals and priorities do change as time passes by.

Thus, it is highly essential to have a keen review of them every monthly. This way, you can assess where you are going and where you've been at this moment.

Actually, there are techniques to use when you want to clarify your present goals. You do not have to prepare many things just to do so. One way is by writing each of your goals down on a sheet of paper.

Separate them into business and personal categories. Ask yourself if each of them is important to you. If one of them is not, remove that sheet of paper and throw it into the trash can. If yes, keep it there.

Techniques

The next thing to do is to ask yourself whether you are willing to do repeated actions to achieve that goal. If no, remove that sheet of paper and discard it. If yes, keep it. Finally, evaluate what you really wish to achieve. Determine how you are going to measure success against that goal and how you can tell if you were able to achieve it. The most critical question is when you want to achieve this goal.

This is a simple activity is also fun and easy to do. It will definitely help you clarify goals not only by being more specific. Do not hesitate to try this action and see how far you can go. After discovering your potential to clarify your goals in life, you can encourage other people to do the same thing.

After mastering the process of setting your goals and overcome all the obstacles in your efforts, then you can handle various goals. Make sure that your goals are achievable. These goals should be challenging and measurable. See to it that you can immediately tell if you observe progress or not.

Aside from that, you need to have general time allotment while achieving the goal. Remember that it may not always be possible to have good control of event timings. You must be able to identify the general time length in which you will achieve your goal. It is always essential to make clarifications on the things you wish to get.

However, do not forget that it is also crucial to have good understanding of the reasons of the need to attain them. There are 5 main questions you need to answer during the process of learning how to clarify goals in life.

- What is my goal?

- Why is it crucial for me to achieve it?

- How can obtaining this goal affect my life?

- What benefits will I experience when I achieved this goal?

- What do I risk losing if I did not obtain my goal?

There have been more available ways to achieve the most effective and best goal setting in life. All you have to do is to make a good choice and informed decisions in all things you do.

Chapter 4

Learn to Put First Things First

Synopsis

You have to be extra careful if you do not have an idea where you are going. This is due to the reason that you may not actually get there. As you reach the time of leaving behind daily stresses and worries of life, you should start defining the successful exit.

Unless you learned setting and prioritizing your exit objectives or goals, you might have many conflicts.

Prioritizing objects helps you pick your whole path. This task is not really easy, however, doing so can provide a frame to proper decision making.

At some points of your life, you might experience waking up one morning knowing that you got a lot of things to do and you do not have an idea where to get started. Most of the time, all things you need to do may seem to be a priority, making it difficult to determine how or where to start.

First Things First!

To make a ball move forward, start somewhere. There are several planning tactics that are helpful enough when it comes to setting your mind on an immediate execution. Even if long term planning and prioritization are also important, the following techniques below will help you experience progress, on a daily micro level basis.

- *Provide a list* – when you wake up every morning, the first thing to do is to take note of the things that are needed to be accomplished within the day. After writing them down, separate such items into non- urgent vs. urgent to distinguish the main priorities for the day.

- *Value assessment* – Complete your tasks and you will get more advantages than others.

- *Honesty* – when your write down the list of your priorities, try to be realistic with your bandwidth. When you set unattainable goals, you will just be disappointed in the end.

- *Flexibility* – to effectively prioritize, you need to deal with those changing priorities. Get them once they come, then decide carefully if they were urgent or not.

- *Cutting the Cord* – For perfectionists, this is actually where they struggle the most. When a particular task is highly essential, it is easy to be caught up. As a result, you spend much time doing that task or project. Acknowledge every time you do this and try to enforce a strict deadline to get rid of getting down a rabbit hole.

Knowing that you have so many things to do every day can definitely make you feel overwhelmed. However, once you start managing them, you can easily prioritize things easier and faster.

Chapter 5

Understand the Win Win Mentality

Synopsis

The world revolving around all the time was established on a premise that human achievement which thrived around and the common thing present in all people is the "Win-win principle". Most cultures have 'win-win' source.

Win-win is just a part of the 6 total human interaction philosophies. Other part of these philosophies include win/lose, win, lose/lose, no deal or win/win, and lose/win. The most suitable model relies on a situation. If relationships have been paramount, this philosophy is just a viable alternative.

5 Dimensions of a Win-Win Model

In competitive situations in which establishing a relationship has not been crucial, win-lose philosophy can be suitable. There are 5 win-win model dimensions which are listed below:

Character

This is the win-win foundation. There should be integrity to build trust in a relationship and define winning when it comes to personal values. The key trait should be abundance mentality where it is present in everybody (scarcity mentality). Abundance mentality comes from the deep personal security and worth inner sense.

Relationships

This is the focus on win-win. Regardless of the type of person you have been dealing with, relationship serves as the key into turning a situation around. When the emotional and trust bank account balances of a relationship are high, there will be a great probability of having a productive and successful interaction.

Performance Agreements

These are also called partnership agreements which provide direction and definition to win-win. They are shifting the production paradigm from vertical (superior to subordinate) going to horizontal (team/partnership). Developing performance agreements has been the central management activity. It allows people manage themselves within the agreement framework.

Reward System

It is the key win-win model element. When an outstanding performance of some people has been rewarded, other members of the team become losers. Instead, try developing team objectives and individual attainable goals to reward.

Process

The process of win-win has 4 main steps:

- Figure out the issue of another point of view; focus on the concerns and needs of other parties.

- Determine the main concerns and issues involved.

- Identify the possible results after making a very acceptable solution.

- Distinguish new choices to obtain the results desired.

You can obtain win-win solutions through win-win procedures. Always remember that win-win mentality has not been the personality technique. This is actually the total human interaction paradigm. It came from the characters of maturity, Abundance mentality and integrity. This grows out of great trust relationships. Win-win has been embodied in the agreements in which it effectively manages and clarifies expectations and accomplishments.

Win-win is seeking for mutual benefits present in the human interactions. It means solutions or agreements have been mutually beneficial. This also serves as a belief which is not "my way" or "your way"; instead, it is "better way", "higher way".

Chapter 6

Learn Empathy

Synopsis

The real great leaders should be empathetic. These people have deep understanding on how to be better at empathy and how to do so. To get started, start with the very basic and analyze the important points carefully.

What is Empathy?

Empathy is an art of perceiving the world just like how somebody else perceives it. If you are empathetic, it only means that you are capable of understanding the feeling of a person in a particular moment and at the same time, understand why such people's actions make sense to him or her.

Empathy allows people to communicate their ideas in the way that are sensible to other people. This has been a part of the building block foundation of greater social interaction as well as powerful and obviously stuff. The good news about it is that it has been the part training and a part talent. Depending on your initial ability level, being good at empathy may require less or more work than somebody else. However, regardless of where you start, you can always educate yourself on how to be more empathetic.

Simple Ways to Learn Empathy

- **Experience Pain** - This is not about living a troubled life. However, when this situation happens, do not ignore it and instead, feel what is happening. Focus on those who are helpful and those who are not. Try to figure out what is something empathetic for you.

- **Reflect and Collect** - Listening along with empathy as you needs to get information first about another person. Know how they feel, what is it about, and why they experience that kind of emotion. After doing so, reflect and make a humble guess on 'where they have been'.

- **Suspend Judgment** – remember that empathy has not been an opinion. Opinions may be required only at certain point. Begin with connection and understanding.

- **Working on Relevant EQ Skills** – examples include understanding non-verbals, listening, thinking or questioning for the perspectives of another person.

- **Practice** – approach certain situations along with deliberate focus when it comes to listening deeply, understanding, reflecting back, and connecting.

The way of expressing empathy has been teachable and the indications of looking for in other people are also teachable. The way to feel other people's needs is also teachable. The ultimate thing that cannot be taught is the "desire" of doing it.

Chapter 7

The Benefits of Being a More Effective Person

Synopsis

People get their self-confidence from you when they had seen that you got confidence in yourself. You should know what to think and not to think.

Always think that you can do and you will succeed in your goals in life. This is where the best confidence starts to come out from your mind and heart. Through effectiveness, your knowledge and skill will grow and from these aspects, you will get confidence. Try new things and make your own self-development plans.

Think about your work more than an occupation. Include enthusiasm, attitude and energy in your daily responsibilities. Pay attention to excellence in every little thing you do. Go beyond your minimum effort, safe path and easy way. Work hard and challenge yourself with something new or different.

The Benefits

Career Learning and Development

It does not matter what particular field you are into. What matters most is your continuous development and learning skills. When you realized the real essence of being an effective person, you will learn that you are doing well in your career. Your personal characteristics will reflect on your daily encounter with your workmates, friends, customers, and other people around.

When you are very effective at your work, you can manage your time well, you communicate clearly, and you got a good attitude. An effective worker has been acknowledged as the most productive and most respected in the workplace.

They are usually the first people considered for promotions. If you are aiming to be recognized as one, then you should strive to achieve effectiveness in all things you do. Once you achieved these things, you will realize that it is worthy to improve your skills in this concept.

Communication Skills

Recall how often you communicate daily. You attend meetings, give presentations, write emails, make calls, talk to clients, and more. Almost all day, you are communicating and connecting with different people around you. That is why excellent communication skills became highly essential especially when the goal is to become more effective at work.

Fortunately, once you start to familiarize your daily routine and apply the necessary solutions, you do not have to worry about other significant aspects.

Having a good communication skill will naturally come out to you as you realize that there is effectiveness in what you do. For this reason, you need to get started in active listening skill development.

It means that you make concerted effort in order to understand and hear what other persons want to tell you. When you already developed good communication and listening skills, you will no longer get easily distracted by different barriers around you.

Productivity and Time Management

The most important thing you need to do to be an effective person at work is by learning time management perfectly. Without managing your time, your days may seem like to have a race daily with phone calls, emails, projects, and other daily tasks you need to prioritize.

Time management and productivity are the two important factors which every person should learn. They are also the keys to a significant and worth living life that is free from stress and worries.

Other benefits that can be received from being a more effective person include the ability to think logically and clearly. Not all people are capable of thinking logically.

However, it can still be developed and acquired to achieve effectiveness. Another possible advantage is the ability to present ideas and structure thoughts effectively and cohesively. As part of the increased confidence level in conducting yourself with external and internal people, you can obtain set of behaviors which have been beneficial at different aspects.

These are only some of the great things that being an effective person can give you. When you know what to do, there is no reason that you can never be highly effective in your daily tasks. You should always take a look at the good side of doing such thing to perceive things well.

Chapter 8

Staying Motivated to be More Effective

Synopsis

Such people find it quite difficult to manage their time and avoid distractions that come along their way. You probably know what to do; however, you cannot make yourself do it. There have been various strategies developed to have a good control of time. In fact, they are obvious enough such as creating a timetable or "To Do" list. So, why don't you try them?

Getting rid of distractions, learn of saying "no", and setting targets can help you do such thing. At the end of the day, only you will be the responsible for your own time management.

Motivation

Setting Goals and Targets

As you explore the ways to become more effective, you should take the path leading you to think about setting targets and your goals in life. First of all, you need to know how to manage time effectively when studying. This way, you already take responsibility.

Next, think about the main reasons why it is a good idea to do such action and where it will end up.

Identify your goals as well as the reward you want to obtain in the near future. It will help you get motivated to become committed in studying or working now.

To know what your targets and goals are, you can make a table divided into three columns. On the first column, try to list your long term goals. On the second column, write about the things to do to fulfill them (medium term goals).

On the last column, write your short term goals to achieve. You can post it on the wall or inside the door of your wardrobe. Mark each goal as you complete them.

Dealing with Distractions

It may be quite difficult to shift your attention to the thing you do when there are many different things that make unpleasant noises or get your attention distractively. However, if you only make yourself be aware of such things that can get you out of focus, you have to think about ways to manage them.

- You will never feel motivated when you think that you always do a particular task. Look for times not to work or study. Try setting an alarm in which you could look for a leisure period to change mode.

- Put things in a silent mode so that you will never be distracted.

- Value yourself as well as your studies or work. Bear in mind that you only have a very short time to do something. Thus, ensure that it will be done right.

- If you want to mix work or studies with other commitments, you cannot really say no to them.

- You deserve giving yourself enough time to show your best.

After learning about simple ways and techniques to stay motivated in all things you do, you will be able to set your principles and develop personal management skill. These will help you view a life that is capable of growing in personal effectiveness and confidence.

Chapter 9

Staying on Track

Synopsis

Motivation starts within you. You may get inspired by those achievements obtained by other people. However, when you go far beyond life, then you will also be determined and charged to reach your goals. Take note of the following tips below on how to get motivated and stay on track with your work, study, and life. These will also keep you going at a top speed to become successful in your career.

Staying On Track

Confidence

When you do not believe in your potentials, nobody else would dare also. People have something in which they are definitely good at. Your faith to yourself is very crucial since it is the way you can try working on the niche skills. Forget about your fear of being a loser in the end of your journey.

Bear in mind that what does not kill you can make you even stronger.

Clarity

It is quite hard to stay on focus when it comes to undefined and fuzzy goals. Try asking for measurable and defined tasks and objectives. Have the initiative to work with the right people if necessary. This way, you will have a clarity regarding your definite roles. Self-motivated persons are working best along with their clearly defined life objectives.

Work Independently

Nothing can work better as the motivation power shot compared to the knowledge that you are excellent in what you are doing. Determine your weaknesses and get rid of them all the way. If you want to get familiar with your tasks, study about them carefully. Remember that there are many available methods that you can use to learn something about them. All you have to do is to look around and be a keen observer all the time.

Positively Take Criticisms

Even if other persons do not have intentions, turn those negative criticisms into positive driving forces. Always bear in mind that failure is just a mind state. When you think of being successful, you will. Think positive. This way, you can route frustration to a positive energy needed to work hard. It serves like magic.

Accept Challenges

When your present job does not motivate you, there is no need to worry. Try to become open for new things if a present role gets boring to pursue another day more. Talk to the experts to help you redefine roles to optimize your abilities.

Persistence

Many things do not really work out at the very first time. It only implies that you should try harder. See to it that your heart is set on your important goals and life progress. Never waste your energy on such peripheral things and save extra efforts for useful things.

Be with Successful People

Stay and talk with confident persons who have been driven on life. Continue reading books that can make you optimistic. Do not forget to meet and deal with successful persons and emulate them.

Chapter 10

Making Resolutions for Being an Effective Person

Resolutions are mostly acknowledged when New Year is coming. People think that it is the only time when they have to make intentions throughout the coming year. The truth is that making a resolution should be a part of your daily life encounter. The fact that many people have their own resolutions in life, most of them cannot fulfill them throughout the year.

There can be challenging resolutions you need to commit and make them a reality. However, when you implement them in your life accordingly, you will understand why you are doing such things. There is actually an easy and fun way to start creating an ideal life along with a little effort. This is called "intention".

Intention

Intention is identifying what you really want in life and directing actions to an outcome. Of course, you want to have a harmonious and peaceful life all the way. Or, you might also crave for discovery and adventure. You have the chance to make intentions for a particular situation or as a whole. You may also create trust and connection with the person you love.

Creating these intentions can take a very short period of time. However, this can be an extremely powerful tool for setting a resolution in motion. You do not have to force yourself just to follow a self-improvement plan or get worried how you are going to accomplish different things. Creating good intentions can remove the worry and effort from this process.

It is definitely difficult to become effective especially if you are not confident. To maintain and establish strong confidence, it is highly essential to say and think of positive things about yourself. Recall your best qualities, thing you had done for other people, and things you already achieved in life.

Forget about worries if you do not have long term goals. In fact, there are only a few people who do so. As you obtain and try more new things, continue pushing yourself out of the comfort zone. Establish effective relationships. Always remember that positive relationship has been the crucial key to reach success. Everybody needs to like and trust you in order to deal with your tasks productively. However, if you really want to get their trust, you have to do and show that you deserve one as well. Be an effective person at your best. Live an inspiring life.

Printed by Libri Plureos GmbH in Hamburg, Germany

9 783476 480453